STREET CAT BOB

Also by James Bowen

A Street Cat Named Bob
The World According to Bob
Bob: No Ordinary Cat
For the Love of Bob
A Gift from Bob
Where in the World is Bob?

STREET CAT BOB

James Bowen

First published in Great Britain in 2015 by Hodder & Stoughton
An Hachette UK company

1

A CIP catalogue record for this title is available from the British Library

Paperback ISBN 978 1 473 60647 0
eBook ISBN 978 1 473 60648 7

Printed and bound by CPI Group (UK) Ltd, Croydon, CR0 4YY

Hodder & Stoughton policy is to use papers that are natural, renewable and recyclable products and made from wood grown in sustainable forests. The logging and manufacturing processes are expected to conform to the environmental regulations of the country of origin.

Hodder & Stoughton Ltd
338 Euston Road
London NW1 3BH

www.hodder.co.uk

To Bryn Fox . . .
and anyone who has lost a friend

Chapter 1
Fellow Travellers

There's a famous quote I read somewhere. It says we are all given second chances every day of our lives. They are there for the taking. It's just that we don't usually take them.

I spent a big chunk of my life proving the truth of that quote. But then, in the early spring of 2007, that finally began to change. It was then that I made friends with Bob. Looking back on it, I see that it might have been his second chance too.

I first met him on a gloomy Thursday evening in March. There was a hint of frost in the air that night when me and my friend Belle arrived back at my new flat in Tottenham, north London, after a day busking around Covent Garden.

The strip lighting in the hallway was broken, but as we made our way to the stair well I noticed a pair of glowing eyes in the gloom.

When I heard a gentle meow I realised what it was.

Edging closer, I could see a ginger cat curled up on a doormat outside one of the ground-floor flats in the corridor that led off the hallway.

I hadn't seen him around the flats before, but even in the darkness I could tell there was something about him. He wasn't at all nervous; in fact, there was a quiet, calm confidence about him. From the shadows he fixed me with a steady, curious, intelligent stare. It was as if he was saying: 'So who are you and what brings you here?'

I couldn't resist kneeling down and greeting him.

'Hello mate. I've not seen you before. Do you live here?'

He just looked at me, as if he was still checking me out.

I stroked his neck, but couldn't feel a collar. Perhaps he was a stray. London had plenty of those.

I could feel that his coat was in a poor state. From the way he was rubbing against me, he was also clearly in need of a bit of tender loving care, or TLC.

'Poor chap. He's really thin,' I said, looking

up at Belle, who was waiting by the foot of the stairs.

She sighed, knowing I had a weakness for cats.

'James, he must belong to whoever lives there,' she said, nodding towards the door of the nearest flat. 'He's probably just waiting for them to come home and let him in. Let's go.'

Reluctantly, I followed her up the stairs. I knew I couldn't just pick up the cat and take it home with me. What if it did belong to the person living in that flat?

Besides, the last thing I needed right now was a pet that needed care. I was a recovering drug addict and failed musician living a hand-to-mouth life in sheltered housing. Taking care of myself was hard enough.

The next morning, I headed downstairs and found the ginger tom still sitting in the hallway.

In the daylight I could see that he was a gorgeous creature. He had a really striking face with piercing green eyes. Looking closer, though, I could tell that he had been in a fight because there were scratches on his face and legs. His coat was very thin and wiry in places with bald patches where you could see the skin. I was now feeling truly concerned about him, but again I told myself that I had more than enough to worry about getting myself sorted out. So, reluctantly, I headed off to catch the bus to Covent Garden to try and earn a few quid busking.

By the time I got back that night it was pretty late. This time there was no sign of the ginger tom. Part of me was disappointed. I'd taken a bit of a shine to him. But mostly I felt relieved. He must have gone home to his owners.

My heart sank when I went down the next day and saw him back in the same place. He looked cold and hungry, and he was shaking a little.

'Still here then,' I said, stroking him. 'Not looking so good today.'

I decided that this had gone on for long enough, so I knocked on the door of the flat.

A guy appeared. He was unshaven, wearing a T-shirt and a pair of track-suit bottoms.

'Sorry to bother you, mate. Is this your cat?' I asked him.

For a second he looked at me as if I was slightly mad. Then he spotted the ginger tom on his doormat.

'No,' he said, with a bored shrug. 'Nothing to do with me.'

Then he slammed the door shut.

I made my mind up there and then.

'OK mate, you're coming with me,' I said.

A few minutes later we were safely settled in my flat. It was pretty threadbare, but after the cold and dark of the corridor it was five-star luxury for the ginger tom.

I got some milk from the fridge, poured it into a saucer and mixed it with a bit of water. He lapped it up in seconds.

I had a bit of tuna, so I mixed it with some mashed up biscuits and gave that to him as well. Again, he ate it fast. *Poor thing, he must be absolutely starving*, I thought.

When I sat down next to him, I saw that he had a big wound on the back of his leg. It looked like he'd been attacked by a dog, or perhaps a fox, that had stuck its teeth into his leg and clung on to him as he'd tried to escape.

I washed the wound as best as I could. A lot of cats would have created havoc, but he was as good as gold as I cleaned it out. He really must have had a hard time of it.

I spent the evening watching my old black and white television, with the tom cat curled up by the radiator. He only moved when I went to bed, picking himself up and following me into the bedroom where he wrapped himself up into a ball by my feet.

As I listened to his gentle purring in the dark, it felt good to have him there. He was company, I guess. I'd not had a lot of that lately.

On Sunday morning I got up quite early and walked the streets to see if anyone had stuck up a 'Lost Cat' poster.

I took the cat with me, on a lead I'd made out of a shoelace. It might have looked a little strange, but he seemed happy to walk by my side as we took the five flights of stairs to the ground floor.

Outside the block of flats the cat began pulling on the string lead as if he wanted to head off. I guessed that he wanted to do his business. Sure enough he went off for a minute or two, then returned to me and happily slipped back into the lead.

He must really trust me, I thought to myself.

It was obvious that he didn't want to leave me. As we wandered around, I couldn't help wondering about his story: where had he come from and what sort of life had he led before he'd come and sat on the mat downstairs?

Cats have a great sense of direction, but maybe he'd been dumped far from home. Or maybe he'd known that it wasn't really home at all and had decided to find a new one.

My other theory was that he'd belonged to an old person who had passed away.

Then again, London has always had a large population of street cats, strays who wander the streets living off scraps and the kindness of strangers. Years ago, places like Gresham Street in the City, Clerkenwell Green and Drury Lane were known as 'cat streets' and were overrun with them. These strays run around fighting for survival every day. They are the rejects of the city, like flotsam and jetsam on the beach. A lot of them were like this ginger tom: slightly battered, broken creatures.

Maybe he'd spotted a kindred spirit in me.

Chapter 2
Road To Recovery

I'd been around cats since I was a child. While I was growing up, my family had several Siamese. At one stage a gorgeous white kitten came to us sick and infested with fleas, but sadly died before we could save it.

I'd thought about that kitten often over the years. She was on my mind a lot that weekend as I spent time with the tom. I could tell he was in a bad state. In fact, I had an awful feeling that he would suffer the same fate as the poor white kitten.

Sitting in the flat with him that Sunday evening, I decided I must take him to a vet.

I set my alarm early and got up to give the cat a bowl of mashed biscuits and tuna. Given the state of his leg, I knew he couldn't manage the ninety-minute walk to the nearest RSPCA centre. So I decided to carry him there in a green recycling box. It wasn't ideal but I couldn't find anything else. As soon as we set off it was clear that he didn't like it. He kept sticking his paw over the top of the box and trying to climb out. Eventually I gave up.

'Come on, I'll carry you,' I said, picking him up with my spare arm. He was soon scrambling up on to my shoulders. I let him sit there while I carried the empty box all the way to the RSPCA centre.

The centre was packed, mostly with dogs and their owners – young teenage blokes with skinhead haircuts and macho tattoos. Most of the dogs were Staffordshire Bull Terriers, many of which looked like they'd been in a fight.

People always talk about Britain as a 'nation of animal lovers'. There wasn't much love on display there, that's for sure.

The cat sat on my shoulder. I could tell he was nervous and I couldn't blame him.

One by one, the snarling dogs were called into the treatment room. In the end it took us four and a half hours to be seen.

Eventually the nurse said, 'Mr Bowen, the vet will see you now.'

He was a middle-aged vet, with a world-weary expression.

I told him how I'd found the cat in the

hallway of my building and pointed out the wound on the back of his leg.

'OK, let's have a quick look at him,' he said.

He could tell the cat was in pain and gave him a small dose of pain killer to help relieve it. He then said that he was going to issue a prescription for a two-week course of cat-strength antibiotics.

'Come back and see me again if things haven't improved in a fortnight,' he said.

He also checked to see if the tom was microchipped, but he wasn't. A microchip would show an owner's address.

'You should get that done when you have a chance,' he said. 'I think he should also be neutered quite soon as well,' he added, handing me a brochure.

Within a few minutes we were finished. Leaving the vet's surgery, I went up to the counter at the dispensary and handed over the prescription.

'He's a lovely looking fellow,' the nurse said. 'My mum had a ginger tom once. Best companion she ever had. Lovely temperament.'

She punched the details into the till and gave me a bill.

'That will be twenty two pounds please, love,' she said.

My heart sank. I had just over thirty pounds in the whole world at that point. But I knew I had no option: I couldn't let my new friend down.

I handed over the cash and spent the change on a bag of cat food.

That night I had to leave the tom on his own in the flat and head to Covent Garden with my guitar. I now had two mouths to feed.

Over the course of the next few days, as I nursed him back to health, I got to know the cat a little better. By then I'd given him a name, Bob, which I got from a character in *Twin Peaks*: Killer Bob. Part of the time he would be a normal, sane guy, but the next moment he would be kind of crazy and out of control. The tom was a bit like that. When he was happy and content, you couldn't have wished to see a calmer, kinder cat. But when the mood took him he could be an absolute maniac, charging around the flat.

As the days passed, Bob became more and more confident and friendly. He could still be very rowdy and even aggressive at times, but by then I knew that was down to the fact that he needed to be neutered.

Our life settled into a bit of a routine. I'd leave Bob in the flat in the morning and head to Covent Garden where I'd play until I got enough cash. When I got home, he'd be waiting for me at the front door. Then he'd sit on the sofa and watch TV with me.

Although I really enjoyed the company of my new furry friend, I knew I had to be careful. I couldn't form too strong a friendship, because sooner or later Bob would want to return to the streets. He didn't seem like the sort of cat that was going to enjoy being cooped up all the time. He wasn't a house cat.

For the short term, however, I was his carer and I was determined to try and fulfil that role to the best of my ability.

The next morning, when I took Bob outside to do his business, he suddenly lunged forward at lightning speed. When he turned around he had a little grey mouse between his teeth.

A lot of people don't like to think of their cute little kitty as a mass murderer, but that's what cats are, given half a chance. In some parts of the world, including Australia, where I grew up, they have strict rules on cats being let out at night, because they kill so many birds and rodents.

It set me thinking again about the life Bob must have led before he arrived in my block of flats. Where had he lived and how had he survived? I would love to have known. I was sure my street cat friend had a tale or two to tell.

In many ways, that was something else that Bob and I had in common.

Ever since I'd ended up living rough on the streets, people had wondered about my past life. How had I landed myself in this position, they'd ask me?

The answer to how people end up on the streets is always different, of course. But there are usually some common factors. Often drugs and alcohol play a big part in the story. But in an awful lot of cases, the road that led them to living on the streets stretches all the way back to their childhoods and to their relationships with their families. That was certainly the way it was for me.

I lived quite a rootless childhood, mainly because I spent it travelling back and forth between the UK and Australia after my parents split up. Life in Australia was pretty good. I had all the space a boy could want to play in, and I loved the Australian landscape. The trouble was that I didn't have any friends.

I found it very hard to fit in at school – mainly, I think, because we moved a lot, never staying anywhere more than a year or two. Then, when I was nine, we moved back to the UK, to Sussex, near Horsham. I was just getting back into life in England when I had to move yet again, back to Western Australia, when I was around twelve.

This time we ended up in a place called Quinns Rock. It was there that I think a lot of my problems really began. At school it was very hard to make friends. I was too eager to impress, which isn't good when you are a kid, and I must have stuck out with my British accent. In fact, I ended up being bullied at every school I went to. It was particularly bad in Quinns Rock.

One day some local bullies decided to stone me. Literally. Quinns Rock had its name for a reason and these kids used all the nice lumps of limestone that were lying around. The attack was so bad that I got concussion.

Things weren't helped by the fact that I didn't get on at all with my stepfather at the time, a guy called Nick – or, as I called him, Nick the

Prick. My mother had met him back in England, and he had come with us out to Australia.

By the time I was in my mid-teens I'd pretty much quit school. I became a tear-away, a wild kid who was always out late, always defying my mother and generally thumbing my nose at authority, no matter what form it took. It wasn't surprising that I soon had a knack of getting myself into trouble, something I have never quite shaken off.

Predictably, I got into drugs, first sniffing glue, then smoking dope. It was all part of a destructive cycle of behaviour. I was angry. I felt like I hadn't had the best breaks.

By the time I was seventeen I had set myself on the road to self-destruction.

My mother tried her hardest to get me off drugs. She went through my pockets and even locked me in my bedroom a few times. But I just learned to pick the locks with a hair pin. I wasn't going to be controlled by her – or anyone else for that matter. We argued even more after that.

Mum was so worried about my mental health at one point that she took me to a doctor – a psychiatrist. They said I had everything from schizophrenia to manic depression to ADHD, or Attention Deficit Hyperactivity Disorder.

Of course, I thought it was all bullshit. Looking back I can see that my mother must have been worried sick. But I was a messed-up teenager who didn't give a damn about other people's feelings.

Around my eighteenth birthday, I announced that I was going to move back from Australia to London. It marked the beginning of my downward spiral.

The plan was that I would stay for six months and pursue my grand dreams of making it as a musician. But things didn't exactly go to plan.

At first, I went to stay with my half-sister in south London. My brother-in-law didn't take too kindly to my arrival. And who'd blame him? I was a rebellious teenager who dressed like a goth and was a complete pain in the arse. And I was paying nothing towards the household bills.

In Australia I'd worked in IT and had sold mobile phones, but back in the UK I couldn't get a decent job. The first I'd been able to get had been as a bartender. But they told me I wasn't right for the job and sacked me. As if that wasn't bad enough, the bar owner then wrote to the dole office saying I'd quit the job, which meant I couldn't collect any benefits for which I might have been eligible.

After that I was even less welcome in my brother-in-law's house. Soon I was kicked out and leading a nomadic life, carrying my sleeping bag with me to various friends' flats and squats around London. Then, when I ran out of floors, I moved to the streets.

Things headed downhill fast from there.

Living on the streets of London strips away your dignity, your identity – your everything, really. Worst of all, it strips away people's opinion of you. They see you are living on the streets and don't want anything to do with you. Soon you haven't got a real friend in the world. While I was sleeping rough, I managed to get a job as a kitchen porter. But they sacked me when they found out I was homeless.

The one thing that might have saved me was going back to Australia. I had a return ticket, but lost my passport two weeks before the flight. I had no papers and, besides, I didn't have the money to get a new passport. Relations with my parents were really bad and, besides, I was too proud to admit that my plans to make a name for myself as a rock star had come to nothing. Any hope I had of getting back to my family in Australia faded. And so, in a way, did I.

The next phase of my life was a fog of drugs, drink, petty crime and, well, hopelessness. It was made worse by my gaining a heroin habit.

I took the drug at first simply to help me get to sleep at night on the streets. It knocked me out and anaesthetised me from the cold and the loneliness. It took me to another place. Sadly, it also took hold of my soul as well. By 1998 I was totally dependent on it. I probably came close to death a few times although, to be honest, I was so out of it at times that I had no idea.

During that period it didn't occur to me to contact anyone in my family. It was as if I had vanished from the face of the earth – and I didn't really care. I was too wrapped up in surviving day to day. Looking back at the time now, I can only imagine that they must have been worried sick.

I had made contact with my father when I'd arrived in London, but hadn't spoken to him in months. It was around Christmas time – nine months into my life on the streets – when I finally gave him a call.

'Where the f*** have you been? We've all been worried sick about you,' he said, when he was calm enough to talk to me.

I made some feeble excuses but he just shouted at me.

He told me that my mother had been in contact with him desperately trying to find out where I was. That was a measure of how worried she'd become, because the two of them never normally spoke. He shouted and screamed at me for fully five minutes. He had probably thought I was dead, which, in a way, I had been.

That period of my life lasted a year or so. I was eventually picked up off the streets by a homeless charity and put on the 'vulnerable housing' list, which gave me priority for sheltered housing. The problem was that for the best part of the next decade I lived in vile hostels and B&Bs, sharing my space with heroin and crack addicts who would steal anything that wasn't nailed down. Everything I had was stolen at some point. I had to sleep with my most important stuff tucked inside my clothes. Survival was all I could think about.

Inevitably, my drug dependency got worse. By the time I was in my late twenties, my habit had got so bad that I ended up in rehab. I spent a couple of months getting sorted and was then put on a drug rehabilitation programme.

It's easy to come up with excuses for drug addiction, but I'm certain I know the reason for mine. It was pure and simple loneliness. I was on my own and, strange as it will seem to most people, heroin was my friend.

Deep down, however, I knew it was killing me – literally. So over a period of a few years I moved off heroin on to its legal substitute, methadone, and hoped eventually to start weaning myself off that and get completely straight.

The move to the flat in Tottenham in north London was part of that process. It was an ordinary block of flats full of ordinary families. I knew I had a chance to put my life back on track there.

To help pay the rent I'd started busking in Covent Garden. It wasn't much, but it helped put food on the table and pay the gas and electricity. It also helped to keep me on an even keel. I knew it was my chance to turn the corner. And I knew I had to take it this time. If I'd been a cat, I'd have been on my ninth life.

Chapter 3
Ticket to Ride

Towards the end of Bob's second week of medication, he was looking a lot brighter. The wound at the back of his leg was healing nicely, and the bald patches on his coat were being replaced with new, thicker fur. He also seemed happier. There was a beautiful green and yellow glow to his eyes that hadn't been there before.

He was getting better and his wild rushing around the flat was the proof of it. There were times when he would jump and run around the place like some kind of maniac. He would claw furiously at everything and anything he could find, including me.

All Bob's actions showed that there was something that needed to be done. He was a young male with way too many hormones flying around his body. There was no doubt that he needed neutering. So, a couple of days before his course of medicine ended, I decided to call the local vets, the Abbey Clinic on Dalston Lane. Luckily they could fit him in.

Bob carried on acting like a whirling dervish. The poor fella had no idea what was coming.

After I dropped him off for the op, I decided to kill time with a spot of busking.

I tried to block Bob out of my thoughts as I played. I didn't want to think about him lying on the operating table. I'd heard stories of cats and dogs going into vets' surgeries for minor procedures and never coming out again.

Time passed very, very slowly. Eventually, however, it was time to pick him up. I almost ran the last few hundred yards to the clinic.

The nurse greeted me with a warm smile.

'How is he? Did it all go all right?' I asked, still breathing heavily.

'He's fine, absolutely fine. Don't worry,' she said. 'Get your breath back and I'll take you through.'

I rushed in and saw Bob lying in a nice warm cage.

'Hello, Bob mate. How you doing?'

He was still very dopey and drowsy, but he

sat upright and started clawing at the doors of the cage as if to say: 'Let me outta here.'

Only then did my heart stop beating wildly. It was weird, I hadn't felt this concerned about someone – or something – for years.

A few weeks later, when Bob had fully recovered, I realised that I had to think about getting him out of the flat and back on to the streets. That's where he had come from – and I assumed that's where he would want to return.

So one morning I took Bob downstairs and out through the hallway. I led him down the path to the gate, and pointed him towards the street.

He just stood there, fixed to the spot, looking at me confused, as if to say: 'What do you want me to do?'

'Go, go, go on,' I said, making sweeping movements with my hands.

That had no effect whatsoever.

For a moment I just stood there, staring at him and he stared back.

It was then that, for the first time, a thought began to take shape in my head.

'I think you want to hang around,' I said quietly to him.

We got into a routine, Bob and I. Each day I'd leave him outside and each night, when I got back from busking, I'd find him waiting for me. One day I headed out for work as usual, with my guitar slung over my shoulder, and Bob started to follow me. I quickly shooed him away.

'Stay there, Bob. You can't come where I'm going.'

He seemed to get the message and he slunk off.

To get to the bus stop I had to cross Tottenham High Road. This morning, as usual, cars, lorries and motor-bikes were tearing down it.

As I stood on the pavement, trying to spot a gap in the traffic, I felt something rub against my leg. Looking down. I saw a familiar creature standing alongside me.

'What the hell are you doing here?' I asked Bob.

He just nudged closer to the edge of the kerb, as if he was about to dart into the road.

I couldn't let him risk it, so I swept him up on my shoulder and carried him across.

'All right, Bob, that's far enough,' I said as I put him down on the pavement and shooed him away again.

A few moments later the bus pulled up. As I got on, I saw a sudden flash of ginger fur. Before I knew it, Bob had jumped up and plonked himself in my lap.

I was amazed. I realised – finally – that I wasn't ever going to shake this cat off.

A moment later, the conductor appeared. She smiled at Bob.

'Is he yours?' she said, stroking him.

'I guess he must be,' I said.

Chapter 4
Centre of Attention

I could feel Bob purring lightly as we walked through the crowd towards Covent Garden. He'd enjoyed the bus journey and now he was happily perched on my shoulder. I couldn't help smiling to myself. I must look a bit like Long John Silver, except I had a puss rather than a parrot sailing along with me.

Then, suddenly, I was aware of something.

Usually, no one would engage, or even exchange a look, with me. I was a busker and this was London, after all. But as I walked down Neal Street that afternoon almost every person we passed was looking at me. Well, more to the point, they were looking at Bob.

It must have looked slightly strange, a tall, long-haired bloke walking along with a large, ginger tom on his shoulders. Not something you see every day – even on the streets of London.

Soon people started stopping us, asking to stroke Bob or take our photo. It made a nice change from being ignored, but it also meant that progress was pretty slow. By the time we got to Covent Garden it was almost an hour after I normally got set up.

'Can't afford to do this every day,' I grumbled to myself.

By then, I'd been busking around Covent Garden for about a year and a half. I generally started at about two or three in the afternoon and carried on until around eight in the evening, to catch people on the way home from work. My main pitch was on a patch of pavement directly outside Covent Garden tube station on James Street.

It could be a bit risky at times. Some people didn't like me approaching them and could be rude and even abusive at times. 'Piss off you scrounger'; 'Get yourself a proper job'. But that was always a part of being a busker. There were also plenty of people who were happy to hear me play a song, then slip me a quid.

Busking at James Street was a bit of a gamble

as well. I was supposed to be on the eastern side of Covent Garden, near the Royal Opera House and Bow Street. James Street was meant to be the place for the human statues. But it was normally free, so I had made it my own little patch.

I knew there was always the risk of getting moved along by the Covent Guardians. It was their job to police the Piazza and make sure the buskers and other entertainers had the right permits to perform – but I took my chances and it usually paid off. Huge numbers of people came out of the tube station. If only one in a thousand of them made a 'drop', then I could do OK.

Arriving at the pitch, I first checked to make sure the coast was clear. There was no sign of the Covent Guardians. There were a couple of people who worked at the tube station who sometimes gave me hassle, because they knew I wasn't supposed to be there. But they didn't seem to be around either. So I put Bob down on the pavement near the wall and unzipped my guitar case.

Usually it would be a good ten minutes before people started to pay attention.

Today though a couple of people slowed down in front of me and lobbed coins into my guitar case even before I'd played a note.

Behind me I heard a male voice. 'Nice cat, mate.'

I turned and saw a guy giving me a thumbs-up sign.

I was taken aback. Bob had curled himself up in a comfortable ball in the middle of the empty guitar case and was already attracting a fair bit of silver.

I knew he was a charmer, but this was something else.

I'd taught myself to play the guitar when I was a teenager in Australia. I got my first guitar when I was fifteen or sixteen from a Cash Converters shop in Melbourne. I loved Jimi Hendrix and wanted to play just like him.

The set I'd put together for my busking featured my heroes: Nirvana, Bob Dylan and a bit of Johnny Cash. The most popular song in my set was 'Wonderwall' by Oasis. That always worked best, especially outside the pubs when I wandered around later in the evenings.

I'd barely been playing for more than a few minutes when a group of Brazilian kids stopped. One of them bent down and began stroking Bob.

'Ah, *gato bonito*,' she said.

'She is saying you have a beautiful cat,' one of the boys translated.

About half a dozen of the Brazilian kids and other passers-by began fishing around in their pockets and started dropping coins into the bag.

I smiled at Bob.

'Looks like you may not be such a bad companion after all.'

As the late afternoon turned into the early evening and the crowds grew, more and more people were slowing down and looking at Bob. There was clearly something about him that attracted people.

As darkness began to fall, a middle-aged lady stopped for a chat.

'You've found yourself a real friend there,' she said, stroking his fur.

'I think you're right,' I smiled.

She placed a fiver in the guitar case before leaving.

I had been used to making around twenty

pounds a session, which was enough to cover my expenses for a few days. But that night, it was clear that I'd made a lot more than that.

When I finally totted it all up, I shook my head quietly. I had made the princely sum of £63.77. To most of the people that might not have seemed like a lot of money. But it was to me.

I put all the coins in my rucksack and hauled it on to my shoulders. It was rattling like a giant piggy bank! I was ecstatic. That was the most I'd ever made in a day's work on the streets: three times what I'd make on a normal day.

I picked up Bob, giving him a stroke on the back of the neck.

'Well done, mate,' I said. 'That was what I call a good evening's work.'

With the money we'd made I treated Bob to a nice pouch of posh cat food, a couple of packs of his favourite nibbles and some cat milk. I also treated myself to a curry and a couple of nice cans of lager.

'Let's push the boat out, Bob,' I said to him. 'It's been a day to remember.'

When we got home, Bob and I both wolfed down our food at lightning speed. I hadn't eaten so well in months – well, maybe years. I'm pretty sure he hadn't either.

Chapter 5
One Man and His Cat

There had been a time when I'd hoped to make it as a real musician. I'd dreamed of becoming the next Kurt Cobain. As naive as it sounds now, it had been part of my grand plan when I'd come back to England from Australia.

That's what I'd told my mother and everyone else when I'd set off.

For a short time, I felt as if I might actually get somewhere.

Around 2002, I'd got off the streets and was living in some sheltered housing in Dalston, east London. I'd formed a band with some guys I'd met, a four-piece guitar band called Hyper Fury, which told you a lot about my state of mind at the time. I was an angry young man. My music was an outlet for my anger and angst.

For that reason we weren't very mainstream. We managed to release two albums. They sold a few copies, but didn't really catch on. Put it this way: we didn't get booked for Glastonbury.

We did have some fans, though, and managed to get some gigs. Things were going so well for us at one point that I teamed up with a guy called Pete and we started our own record label, Corrupt Drive Records.

But it didn't really work – or to be honest, I didn't really work.

At the time my best friend Belle and I were seeing each other. We got on great as friends, but as a relationship it was kind of doomed from the beginning. The problem was that she was on drugs as well. When one of us was trying to get clean, the other one was using – and vice versa. That's what is called co-dependency.

By 2005 I was struggling so badly with my habit that I fell by the wayside – again. It became another of those second chances that I let slip through my fingers. I guess I'll never know what might have been.

I never gave up on music, however. Even when the band broke up and it was clear that I wasn't going to get anywhere with it as a career, I would spend hours most days playing on the guitar, improvising songs. It was a great outlet for me. God knows where I'd have been without it. And busking had certainly made a difference to my life in recent years. Without it, I dread to think what I would have ended up doing to earn cash. That really doesn't bear thinking about.

After that first day, Bob would come along when I headed out to work and keep me company. He was always the centre of attention. I loved the way that Bob seemed to be able to brighten up people's days.

He was a beautiful creature. There was no doubt about that. But it wasn't just that. There was something else about Bob. He had an unusual way with people. He was special.

It was during the third week of us busking together that he first decided he didn't want to join me. Usually, the minute he saw me putting on my coat and packing my rucksack, he'd be moving towards me, ready for me to put his lead on. But then, one day, as I went through the normal routine, he just shuffled off behind the sofa for a bit, then went and lay down under the radiator. It was as if to say 'I'm having a day off.'

'Don't fancy it today, Bob?'

He looked at me in that knowing way of his.

'No problem,' I said, waving goodbye.

Going out that day really showed me the difference Bob had made to my life. With him on my shoulder or walking on the lead in front of me, I turned heads everywhere. On my own I was invisible again. By now we were well-known enough for a few people to express concern.

'Where's the cat today?' one local stall-owner asked.

'He's having a day off.'

'Oh, good. I was worried something had happened to the little fella,' he smiled, giving me the thumbs-up.

Without Bob, I didn't make anywhere near as much money busking. It took me hours to earn even half the cash we made on a good day together.

But it was only as I walked back that evening that something began to sink in. It wasn't about the money. It was about my life being much richer for having Bob in it.

It was such a pleasure to have such a great

companion. Somehow it felt like I'd been given a chance to get back on track.

It's not easy when you're working on the streets. People don't want to give you a chance. Before I had Bob I would try to approach people in the pubs and they would go 'no, sorry' before I'd even had a chance to say hello.

People don't want to listen. All they see is someone they think is trying to get a free ride. They don't see that you're working, not begging. Just because I'm not wearing a suit and a tie and carrying a briefcase, doesn't mean that I'm free-loading.

Having Bob there gave me a chance to interact with people.

They would ask about Bob and I would get a chance to explain myself at the same time. They would ask where he came from, and I'd then be able to explain how we got together and how we were making money to pay our rent, food, electricity and gas bills. People would give me more of a fair hearing.

People also began to see me in a new way.

Seeing me with my cat softened me in their eyes. It humanised me. In some ways it was giving me back my identity. I had been a non-person. I was becoming a person again.

Chapter 6
The Two Musketeers

Bob wasn't just changing people's view of me: he was changing my view of others as well.

I'd never really had any responsibilities towards anyone else. I'd had the odd job here and there and I'd been in the band, but the truth was that, since I left home as a teenager, my main responsibility had always been to myself. I'd always had to look after number one, simply because there wasn't anyone else to do it. As a result, my life had become a very selfish one. It was all about my day-to-day survival.

Bob's arrival in my life had totally changed all that. Suddenly, another being's health and happiness were down to me.

It was really rewarding, but it was scary too.

I worried about Bob all the time, especially when I was out on the streets. I was always ready to protect him; my instincts were telling me that I had to watch out for him at every turn. With good cause.

I wasn't lulled into a false sense of security by the way people treated me and Bob. The streets of London aren't all filled with kind-hearted tourists and cat lovers. Not everyone was going to react the same way when they saw a long-haired busker and his cat singing for their suppers on street corners. It happened less now that I had Bob, but I still got a storm of abuse every now and again, usually from drunken young blokes.

'Get off your arse and do a proper day's work, you long-haired layabout,' they would say, usually in more colourful language than that.

I let their insults wash over me. But it was a different matter when people turned their aggression on Bob. That's when my instinct to protect him really took over.

A month or so after Bob and I had first come to Covent Garden together, I was busking on James Street when a bunch of young, very rowdy lads came past. They seemed angry and were obviously on the look-out for trouble. A couple of them spotted Bob sitting on the pavement next to me and started making 'woof' and 'meow' noises, much to the amusement of their mates.

Then one of them kicked the guitar case, sending the case – and Bob, who was sitting in it – sliding along the pavement.

Bob leapt out and hid behind my rucksack.

I got up like a shot and confronted the guy.

'What the f*** did you do that for?' I said, standing toe-to-toe with him.

'I just wanted to see if the cat was real,' he said, laughing as if he'd cracked a brilliant joke.

I didn't see the funny side.

'That's really clever, you f****** idiot,' I said.

That was the signal for it all to kick off. They all began circling me and one of them shoved into me with his chest and shoulders, but I stood my ground and shoved him back. For a second or two there was a stand-off, but then I pointed to a nearby CCTV camera.

'Go on then, do what you want. But just remember: you're on camera.'

They had to back off after that, but I didn't hang around much longer that evening. I knew their type. They wouldn't take kindly to being dissed.

The clash reminded me of something I'd already known. I really was on my own when trouble flared like this. There wasn't a police officer in sight. There wasn't a sign of a Covent Guardian. Although quite a lot of people were milling around when the gang circled me, none of them tried to help. In fact, people did their best to melt into the background. Nobody was going to come to my aid. In that respect, nothing had changed. Except, of course, now I had Bob.

As we headed back up to Tottenham on the bus that evening, he cosied up to me. 'It's you and me against the world,' I said to him. 'We're the two Musketeers.'

He nuzzled up to me and purred lightly, as if in agreement.

The hard reality was that London was full of people we had to treat with caution.

A week or two later we were sitting in Neal Street when a guy with a Staffordshire Bull Terrier loomed into view. He was shaven-headed, swigging extra-strength lager and wearing a tatty tracksuit. From the way he was swaying around in the street, he was off his head already, even though it was barely 4 p.m.

They slowed down when they got to us because the Staff was straining at the leash, sniffing round Bob and his cat biscuits.

I couldn't believe what happened next.

As the Staffie leaned in towards the biscuits, Bob calmly looked up and then just bopped the dog on the nose with his paw. It was so lightning fast, it was a punch to do Muhammad Ali proud.

The dog couldn't believe it. He just jumped back in shock and then carried on backing off.

I was almost as shocked as the dog, I think. I just laughed out loud.

What the Staffie couldn't have known was that Bob was always funny about his food. Although I was feeding him regularly, he still treated every meal as if it was going to be his last. At home in the flat, the moment I scooped some cat food into his bowl he would stick his face in it and start guzzling as fast as he could.

'Slow down and enjoy your food, Bob,' I'd tell him, but he took no notice. It was as if he wasn't used to knowing where his next meal would come from. I knew how that felt. I'd spent large chunks of my life living the same way.

Bob and I had so much in common. Maybe that was why the bond had formed so fast – and was growing so deep.

Having Bob with me had already made a difference to the way I was living my life. He'd made me clean up my act in more ways than one.

As well as giving me more routine and a sense of responsibility, he had also made me take a good look at myself.

I didn't like what I saw.

I wasn't proud of being a recovering addict and I certainly wasn't proud of the fact that I had to visit a clinic once a fortnight and collect medication from a pharmacy every day. So I made it a rule that, unless I really had to, I wouldn't take him with me on those trips. It may sound crazy, but I didn't want him seeing that side of my past. That was something else he'd helped me with; I really did see it as my past.

There were still plenty of reminders of that past and of how far I had still to travel. One morning I was looking for an old travel card in my bedroom cupboard. There, right at the back, my fingers brushed against a plastic Tupperware box. I recognised it right away, although I hadn't seen it for a while.

It contained all the kit I had collected when I was doing heroin. There were syringes, needles, everything I had needed to feed my habit. It brought back a lot of bad memories – images of myself that I had hoped to banish from my mind forever.

I decided at once that I didn't want that box in the house any more. I didn't want it there to remind and maybe even tempt me. And I definitely didn't want it around Bob.

Bob was sitting next to the radiator as usual, but got up when he saw me putting my coat on and getting ready to go downstairs. He followed me all the way down to the bin area and watched me as I threw the box into a recycling container for hazardous waste.

'There,' I said, turning to Bob who was now fixing me with one of his curious stares. 'Just doing something I should have done a long time ago.'

Chapter 7
Santa Paws

As Christmas 2007 approached and our first year together drew to a close, our life had settled into a real routine. In between our busking gigs, I'd gone ahead and got Bob microchipped and now, more than ever, it felt like we really belonged to one another.

With Christmas only days away, the crowds in Covent Garden were getting bigger and bigger. So too were the number of treats and gifts Bob was getting. From the very early days, people had got into the habit of giving Bob little presents.

One lady had even stitched his name, 'Bob', into a little scarf that she had knitted him. In fact, Bob was becoming quite the fashion model. He was regularly modelling the new clothes some kind soul had made for him. It gave new meaning to the word 'catwalk'.

Clearly I wasn't the only one who was forming

a deep affection for Bob. He seemed to make friends with almost everyone he met. It was a gift I wished I had myself. I'd never found it that easy to bond with people.

No one had fallen more deeply in love with Bob than my ex-girlfriend Belle. We were still close friends and she would pop round to the flat regularly. It was partly to see me and hang out, but I was pretty sure that she was also coming over to see Bob.

The two of them would play together for hours on the sofa. Bob thought the world of her, I could tell.

About three weeks before Christmas she came round with a plastic shopping bag in her hand and a big grin on her face.

'What have you got in there?' I said, sensing she was up to something.

'It's not for you. It's for Bob.'

Bob was sitting in his usual spot under the radiator, but perked up the minute he heard his name.

'Bob, come here. I've got a surprise for you,' Belle said, flopping on to the sofa with the bag. He was soon padding over, curious to find out what was inside.

Belle pulled out a couple of small animal T-shirts. One had the words 'Santa Paws' in large white letters with a big paw print underneath it.

'Oh that's really cool, Bob, isn't it?' I said. 'That will really put a smile on people's faces.'

It certainly did that.

I don't know if it was the Christmas spirit or simply seeing him in his outfit, but the effect was amazing.

'Ah look, it's Santa Paws,' I'd hear people say every few minutes.

A lot of people would stop and drop a bit of silver into my guitar case; others, however, wanted to give Bob something.

One time, a very smart lady stopped and started cooing over Bob.

'He's fabulous,' she said. 'Do you think he'd like something for Christmas?'

'Why not,' I smiled.

I didn't think much more of it, but about an hour later the lady came back. She had a big grin on her face and was carrying a smart-looking hand-knitted stocking with cat designs on the front. I looked inside and could see it was stuffed with goodies: food, toys and stuff.

'You must promise me that you won't open it till Christmas,' she said. 'You must keep it under your tree until Christmas morning.'

I didn't have the heart to tell her that I didn't

have enough money for a Christmas tree or any decorations for the flat.

In the days after that, however, I made a decision. She was right. I should have a decent Christmas for once. This year I had something to celebrate: I had Bob.

For a long time now, I'd been one of those people who dreaded Christmas.

During the past decade or so I'd spent most of them at places like Shelter, where they did a big Christmas lunch for homeless people. It was all very well-meaning and I'd had a laugh or two there. But it just reminded me of what I didn't have: a normal life and a normal family. It just reminded me that I'd messed up my life.

This year was different though. I invited Belle round on Christmas Eve for a drink. Then for Christmas Day I splashed out on turkey breast with all the trimmings. I also got Bob some really nice treats, including his favourite chicken meal.

When Christmas Day came we got up early and went out for a short walk so that Bob could do his business. There were other families from our block heading off to see relatives and friends. We greeted each other with 'Happy Christmas' and smiles. Even that was more than I'd heard and seen in a long while.

Back up at the flat, I gave Bob his stocking. He had spotted it days earlier and had obviously guessed it was meant for him. I emptied the contents one by one. There were treats, toys, balls and little soft things filled with catnip. He absolutely loved it all and was soon playing with his new toys, exactly like an excitable child would be doing on Christmas morning. It was pretty adorable.

I cooked our lunch early in the afternoon. Then I put a hat on each of us, had a can of beer and watched television. It was the best Christmas I'd had in years.

Chapter 8
Mistaken Identity

By the spring and summer of 2008, being a busker on the streets of London was becoming more and more difficult.

I know people assume the economy doesn't affect people on the streets, but that's not true at all. The recession had hit me and people like me quite hard. The kind-hearted folk who used to think nothing of dropping me and Bob a pound or two were now holding on to their money. One or two regulars even told me as much. They said they were worried about losing their jobs. I couldn't really argue with that. But, as a result, I was having to work much longer hours in order to feed me and Bob and keep us warm.

I could live with that. The bigger problem was that the authorities had started coming down hard on street performers who didn't work in the spots they were supposed to.

It had become a constant game of 'hide and

seek' and I was running out of places to hide. If it wasn't the Covent Guardians, it was the British Transport Police, wanting to move me on. For the most part it wasn't nasty – just people doing their jobs.

All that changed one afternoon.

I'd headed into Covent Garden as usual with Bob. I had a friend staying with me at the time, a guy called Dylan, who I'd met way back when I was with the band.

This particular afternoon Dylan decided he was going to come into central London with us and hang around Covent Garden. It was a lovely, sunny day and he felt like enjoying it. He was playing with Bob as I set myself up on the corner of James Street. Looking back, I can't believe how lucky it was that he was there.

I'd barely put the guitar strap over my shoulder when a British Transport Police van arrived at speed and pulled up beside the pavement. Three officers jumped out and started walking towards me.

'What's all this about?' Dylan asked.

'Don't know. More of the usual stuff,' I said,

fully expecting to have to go through the same old routine.

I was wrong.

'Right you, you're coming with us,' one of the officers said, pointing at me.

'What for?' I asked.

'We're arresting you on suspicion of using threatening behaviour.'

'What? Threatening who? What the hell—'

Before I could finish my sentence they had grabbed me. While one of them read me my rights, another one stuck me in handcuffs.

'We'll explain at the station. Get your stuff together and get in the van before we make things even worse for you,' he said.

'What about my cat?' I said gesturing at Bob.

'We've got some dog kennels at the station. We'll stick him in there,' another of the officers said. 'Unless you've got someone to take him.'

My head was spinning.

'Dylan, will you look after Bob?' I said. 'Take him back to the flat. The keys are in my rucksack.'

He nodded. As I was hustled into the police van, I watched him scoop Bob up and reassure him. I could see the look on Bob's face; he was terrified by what was happening to me. Through the mesh windows at the back of the van, I watched as Dylan and Bob disappeared from my view.

We drove to the British Transport Police station. I still had no idea what was going on.

Within a few minutes, I was led into a cell where I was told to wait until I was seen by an officer. As I sat there in the cell, the walls scratched with graffiti and the floor smelling of stale urine, awful memories flooded back.

I'd had run-ins with the police before, mostly for petty theft.

When you're homeless or have a drug habit you try to find easy ways to make money. And, to be honest, few things are easier than shoplifting. My main thing was stealing meat. I'd lift legs of lamb and expensive steaks. Jamie Oliver steaks. Lamb shanks. Gammon joints. Never chicken, chicken is too low value. What you get is half the price on the label. If you go to a pub and sell the stuff, that's what you could expect to get. Pubs are very solid ground for selling stolen goods. Everybody knows that.

The first time I did it to pay for my habit was around 2001 or 2002. I'd been moved into some dodgy housing where everyone was using drugs, and I had fallen back into bad habits.

I can still remember the first time I got busted. It was at Marks & Spencer in Islington. I used to dress up smartly and tie my hair back, hoping to look like a postman at the end of his daily round popping in for a pint of milk on the way home. It was all about how you looked. If I'd walked in with a rucksack or a shopping bag, I'd never have stood a chance. I carried a postman's Royal Mail bag around with me. Nobody looked twice at you if you had one of those bags slung over your shoulders.

Anyhow, I got stopped one day. I had about £120-worth of meat on me.

I was taken into police custody and given an on-the-spot fine. I was lucky – it was my first time getting nicked.

Of course, it didn't stop me. I had a habit. I was on heroin and a bit of crack now and then. You take the risk. You have to.

When you get nicked it feels awful. You try to get out of it. You make up lies but they don't believe you. They never do. It's a vicious circle when you're down.

That was why busking had been so good for me. It was legal. It kept me straight. But now here I was back in the nick. It felt like a real kick in the stomach.

I'd been in the cell for about half an hour when the door opened suddenly and a white-shirted officer ushered me out.

'Come on,' he said.

'Where are you taking me now?' I asked.

'You'll see.'

I was taken into a bare room with a few plastic chairs and a single table.

There were a couple of bored-looking officers sitting facing me.

'Where were you yesterday evening at around 6.30 p.m?' one of them asked.

'Um, I was busking in Covent Garden.'

'Where?'

'On the corner of James Street, opposite the entrance to the tube,' I said, which was true.

'Did you go into the tube station at any time that evening?' the copper asked.

'No, I never go in there,' I said. 'I travel by bus.'

'Well, how come we've got at least two witnesses saying that you were in the station and that you verbally abused and spat at a female ticket attendant?'

That was it; I lost my cool.

'Look, this is bullshit,' I said. 'I told you I wasn't in the tube station last night. I'm never in there. And I never travel by tube. Me and my cat travel everywhere by bus.'

They just looked at me as if I was telling the biggest lies in the world.

They asked me if I wanted to make a statement, so I did, explaining that I'd been busking all night. I knew the CCTV footage would back this up. But at the back of my mind I was having all sorts of paranoid thoughts.

What if it was a fit up? What if it went to court and it was my word against three or four London Underground officers?

Worst of all, I found myself fretting about what would happen to Bob. Who would look after him?

They kept me at the station for another three hours or so. After a while I lost all track of time. There was no natural light in the room, so I had no idea whether it was day or night outside. At one point a lady police officer came in with a surly-looking male officer behind her.

'I need to do a DNA test,' she said, while he stood with his arms folded, glaring at me.

'OK,' I said, ignoring him. 'What do I have to do?'

'Just sit there and I'll take a swab of saliva from your mouth.'

She pulled out a little kit filled with loads of swabs and test tubes.

Suddenly I felt like I was at the dentist.

'Open wide,' she said.

She then stuck a long, cotton bud into my mouth, gave it a bit of a scrape around the inside of my cheek and that was that.

'All done,' she said, putting the bud in a test tube and packing her stuff away.

Eventually I was let out. I had to sign a form saying that I was released on bail, and they told me that I had to return in a couple of days.

'When will I know if I am being formally charged?' I asked the duty officer.

He said that I'd probably know when I came back in a couple of days' time.

That was good and bad, I decided. Good in the sense that I'd not have to wait months to find out if I was going to be charged; bad in the sense that, if they did charge me, I could find myself spending time inside very soon.

I felt powerless, angry – and really scared.

In the end there was good news and there was bad news. The good news was that I wasn't going to be charged with threatening behaviour.

'The DNA didn't match the saliva on the

ticket collector's booth did it?' I asked the police officer.

He just looked at me with a tight-lipped smile. Then he told me the bad news: I was being charged with illegally busking, or 'touting for reward' to give it its formal title, and I had to report to court in a week's time.

A week later, I put on a clean shirt, took a deep breath, and pleaded guilty to the charges against me.

Belle and Bob were waiting for me outside the courthouse after the hearing was over. Bob immediately jumped off her lap and walked over to me. It was clear he was pleased to see me.

'How did it go?' Belle asked.

'Three-month conditional discharge, but if I get caught again I'm for the high jump,' I said.

'So what are you going to do?'

I looked at her, then looked down at Bob. The answer must have been written all over my face.

I had reached the end of the road. I'd been busking on and off now for almost ten years. Times had changed and my life had changed, certainly since Bob had come into it. There were times when busking didn't earn me enough money to make ends meet. There were times when it put me – and more importantly, Bob – in danger. Maybe even in jail.

'I don't know what I'm going to do, Belle,' I said. 'But the one thing I know I'm not going to do is carry on busking.'

Chapter 9
Number 683

My head was spinning for the next few days. I felt a real mixture of emotions.

Deep down I knew I wasn't going to turn my life around singing Johnny Cash and Oasis songs on street corners. I wasn't going to build up the strength to get myself totally clean by relying on my guitar. It began to dawn on me that I was at a big crossroads, and that I had a chance to put the past behind me. I'd been there before, but for the first time in years I felt like I was ready to take that chance.

That was all very well in theory, of course. I also knew the brutal truth: my options were pretty limited. How was I going to earn money? Who was going to give me a job?

I realised quickly that there was only one realistic alternative to busking. I didn't have the time to wait for something to turn up. I needed to make money to look after myself and

Bob. So a couple of days after the court hearing I set off with Bob for Covent Garden – for the first time in years, without my guitar on my back. When I got to the Piazza, I headed for the spot where I knew I'd find a girl called Sam, the area's *The Big Issue* co-ordinator.

I had tried selling *The Big Issue* magazine before, back in 1998 when I first ended up on the streets. I'd got myself accredited and worked the streets around Charing Cross and Trafalgar Square. It didn't work out. I lasted less than a year before I gave it up.

I could still remember how difficult it was. So many people used to come up to me and snarl 'Get a job!' That used to really upset me. They didn't realise that selling *The Big Issue* is a job. In fact, being an official seller in effect means you're running your own business. When I was selling the magazine I had costs. I had to buy copies to sell. So each day I turned up at the co-ordinator's stand I had to have at least a few quid in order to buy a few copies of the magazine. You had to have money to make money.

The philosophy of The Big Issue Foundation is to help people to help themselves. But, back then, I wasn't really sure I wanted any help. I wasn't ready for it.

I could still remember some of the grim,

soul-destroying days I'd spent sitting on a wet and windy street corner pitch, trying to coax Londoners to part with their cash in return for a magazine. It was really hard, especially as back then my life was still ruled by drugs. All I usually got for my trouble was a load of abuse.

Most of all it had been hard because I had been invisible. Most people just didn't look at me. They would do all they could to avoid me, in fact. That's why I had turned to busking. At least then I had my music to attract people's attention and let them know I was a living, breathing creature.

I wouldn't have even thought about going back to selling *The Big Issue* if it hadn't been for Bob. The way he'd changed my fortunes – and my spirits – on the streets had been amazing. If I could do as well selling *The Big Issue* as I'd done busking with Bob, then maybe I could take that big step forward. Of course there was a problem: I had to get them to accept me first.

I found Sam at the spot where the area's *The Big Issue* sellers met to buy their magazines, on a side street off the main Piazza of Covent Garden. There were a few sellers there, all men.

'Hello. You two not busking today?' Sam said, giving Bob a friendly pat.

'No. I'm going to have to knock that on the head,' I said. 'Bit of trouble with the cops. If I get caught doing it illegally again, I'm going to be in big trouble. Can't risk it now I've got Bob to look after. Can I, mate? So,' I said, rocking up and down on my heels, 'I was wondering—'

Sam smiled and cut me off.

'Well, it all depends on whether you meet the criteria.'

'Oh yeah, I do,' I said, knowing that as a person in what was known as 'vulnerable housing' I was eligible to sell the magazine.

'Right then. You just need to get down to Vauxhall to sign up.'

The next day I made myself look decent, tied my hair back and set off for Vauxhall.

I took Bob with me. He was going to be part of my team, so I wanted to get him signed up as well, if that was possible.

The Big Issue offices are in an ordinary-looking office block on the south side of the Thames, near Vauxhall Bridge and the MI6 building.

The first thing I saw when I arrived in the reception area was a large sign saying 'No Dogs

Allowed'. Luckily it didn't say anything about cats.

After filling in a few bits of paper, I was called in to have an interview. The guy was a decent bloke and we chatted for a while. He'd been on the streets himself years ago, and had sold the magazine as a stepping-stone to help get his life together.

I explained my circumstances. He seemed to understand.

'I know what it's like out there, James, believe me,' he said.

It took just a few minutes before he gave me a thumbs-up sign and told me to go and get my badge in another office.

I had to have my photo taken and then wait to get a laminated badge with my vendor number on it. I asked the guy who was issuing the badges whether Bob could have an ID card as well.

'Sorry,' he said, shaking his head. 'Pets aren't allowed to have their own badges. We've had this before with dogs. Never with a cat, though.'

'Well, what about if he is in the picture with me?' I asked.

He pulled a face. But in the end he agreed.

'Go on then.'

'Smile, Bob,' I said, as we sat in front of the camera.

After we'd waited about a quarter of an hour, the guy came back.

'Here you go, Mr Bowen,' he said, handing me the laminated badge.

I couldn't help breaking into a big grin at the picture. Bob was on the left-hand side. We were a team. *The Big Issue* Vendor Number 683.

It was a long journey back to Tottenham, so I began reading through the little booklet they gave me.

It began with the magazine's main philosophy:

> The Big Issue exists to offer homeless and vulnerably housed people the opportunity to earn a legitimate income by selling a magazine to the general public. We believe in offering 'a hand up, not a hand out' and in enabling individuals to take control of their lives.

That's exactly what I want, I said to myself, *a hand up. And this time I'll accept it.*

Starting out with a trial pitch, I'd get ten free copies of the magazine to get me started. The booklet made it clear that it was then down to me:

> Once they have sold these magazines they can purchase further copies, which they buy for £1 and sell for £2, thereby making £1 per copy.

That was the simple economics of it. But there was a lot more to it than that, as I would soon find out.

The next day, when Sam pointed me towards my trial pitch, I couldn't stop myself from bursting out laughing. It was right next to my old spot on James Street.

'Are you OK? Is that a problem?' she said, looking worried.

'No,' I said. 'It'll be great there. It'll be a real walk down memory lane. I'll get started right away.'

I wasted no time and set up quickly. It was a bright, sunny morning which, I knew from my busking days, always puts people in a more generous mood.

When I'd been busking, I'd always felt like I was in danger of hassle from the authorities by playing here. Selling *The Big Issue* was totally different. I was officially allowed to be there. So I stood as close to the station as possible.

Then I got on with the job of trying to shift my ten copies.

For other sellers the pitch would have been a nightmare – people rushing in and out of the tube, much too busy to stop and chat. But I had a secret weapon, one that had already cast his spell on Covent Garden. And he was soon weaving his magic.

Within moments of me setting up, a couple of young American tourists had stopped and started pointing at Bob.

'*Aaaah,*' one of them said, reaching for her camera.

'Do you mind if we take a picture of your cat?' the other one asked.

'Sure, why not?' I said. 'Would you like to buy a copy of *The Big Issue* while you're at it?'

Sure enough, I sold six copies within the first hour. Most people gave me the correct money, but one elderly gent in a smart tweed suit gave me a fiver. It had been a pretty good day already, but it got even better when a large, sweaty ticket attendant spotted me and Bob outside the station. Right away he marched in our direction.

'What the hell are you doing here?' he said. His face was as red as a beetroot. 'I thought you'd been locked up. You know you're not supposed to be here.'

Very slowly and deliberately, I flashed him my vendor's badge. 'I'm just doing my job, mate,' I said, greatly enjoying the mixture of confusion and anger spreading across his face. 'I suggest you get on with yours.'

Chapter 10
Pitch Perfect

I hadn't got many things right in my life. Whenever I'd been given a chance in the past ten years, I'd screwed things up big time. Within a couple of days of deciding to sell *The Big Issue*, however, I was pretty sure that I'd taken a step in the right direction for once.

Being with Bob had already taught me a lot about responsibility but my new job took that to another level. If I wasn't responsible and organised, I didn't earn money. And if I didn't earn money, Bob and I didn't eat. So from that very first fortnight, I had to learn how to run my pitch as a business.

Buy too many magazines and you were screwed, as there was no such thing as sale or return. Buy too few and you'd sell out too quickly and miss out on willing buyers.

It took a while to get the balance right.

With Bob at my side I found that I could sell

as many as thirty or even fifty magazines on a good day. At £2 a copy, as they were priced back then, it could add up quite well, especially with the tips that some people gave me – or, more usually, Bob.

Of course, not everyone was thrilled about how well Bob and I were doing. There was a bit of trouble from the older vendors, and once I even found myself suspended for what they saw as muscling in on their pitch. I managed to calm them down, but for a while it looked a bit touch and go.

But while being put on the 'naughty list' shook me up a bit, it was nothing compared to Bob getting sick.

I noticed it first one rainy day, when we were walking through Covent Garden. Bob was sat on my shoulder, as usual.

All of a sudden he began moving in a really agitated way, making weird retching noises as if he was choking or trying to clear his throat. I was sure he was going to jump or fall off, so I put him down on the street to see what was wrong. But before I could even kneel down he began to vomit. I could see his body shaking as he retched.

'It's all right, Bob,' I said, stroking his fur. 'Everything will be okay.'

But I wasn't sure if I really believed that.

As he lay on my lap on the bus back home to Tottenham, I felt the emotions welling up. It was hard to stop myself bursting into tears. Bob was the best thing in my life. The thought of losing him was terrifying. I couldn't keep that thought out of my head.

When we got home, Bob headed straight for the radiator where he just curled up and went to sleep. He stayed there for hours. That night I didn't sleep much, worrying about him. I'd sneak out of bed, just to check he was still breathing.

Next morning I called up Rosemary, a veterinary nurse I knew through my mate Steve. I must have sounded desperate, but she managed to calm me down.

'Probably just eaten something nasty,' she assured me. 'I'll send over some antibiotics and something to settle his stomach. He'll be fine in no time.'

Bob didn't like the taste of the medicine. He screwed his face up and took half a step back when I gave him his first spoonful of it.

'Tough luck, mate,' I said. 'If you didn't stick your face in rubbish bins, you wouldn't have to take this stuff.'

The medicine had an almost immediate impact, but seeing Bob sick had an equally profound effect on me. He had seemed to be such a tough, fit cat. I'd never imagined him getting ill. Finding out that he was mortal really shook me.

It boosted the feeling that had been building inside me for a while now. It was time for me to get myself clean.

I was fed up with having to go to the DDU – Drug Dependency Unit – every fortnight, and the chemist every day. I was tired of feeling like I could slip back into addiction at any time.

So the next time I went to see my counsellor I asked him about coming off methadone, and taking the final step towards becoming completely clean. We'd talked about it before, but I don't think he'd ever really believed me. Today, he could tell I was serious.

'Won't be easy, James,' he said.

'Yeah, I know that.'

'You'll need to take a drug called Subutex. We can then slowly decrease the dosage of that, so that you don't need to take anything.'

'OK.'

'The transition can be hard. You can have quite severe withdrawal symptoms,' he said, leaning forward.

'That's my problem,' I said. 'But I want to do it. I want to do it for myself and for Bob.'

For the first time in years, I felt like I could see the tiniest light at the end of a very dark tunnel.

Chapter 11

Forty-eight Hours

The young counsellor at the DDU scribbled his name at the bottom of the prescription and handed it to me with a stern look on his face.

'Remember, take this, then come back to me at least forty-eight hours later when you can feel the withdrawal symptoms have really kicked in,' he said, staring into my eyes. 'It's going to be tough, but it will be a lot tougher if you don't stick to what I've said. OK?'

I nodded, picking myself up and heading out of his treatment room. 'Just hope I can do it.'

The prescription the counsellor had just given me was for my last dose of methadone. Methadone had helped me kick my dependence on heroin. But I'd now reduced my usage to such an extent that it was time to stop taking it for good.

When I next came to the DDU in a couple of days' time, I would be given my first dose of a much milder medication, Subutex, which would ease me out of drug dependency completely. The counsellor described the process as like landing an aeroplane, which I thought was a good analogy. In the months ahead he would slowly cut back my dosage until it was almost zero. As he did so, he said, I would slowly drop back down to earth, landing – hopefully – with a very gentle bump.

As I waited for the prescription to be made up, I thought about what lay ahead during the next forty-eight hours.

The counsellor had explained the risk to me in graphic detail. Coming off methadone wasn't easy. I'd suffer 'clucking' or 'cold turkey', a series of nasty physical and mental withdrawal symptoms. I had to wait for those symptoms to become quite severe before I could go back to the clinic to get my first dose of Subutex. If I didn't, I risked having what's known as a precipitated withdrawal. This is basically a much worse withdrawal. It didn't bear thinking about.

But reality had finally dawned on me. I'd been living this way for ten years. A lot of my life had just slipped away. I'd wasted so much time, sitting around watching the days vanish. When you're dependent on drugs, minutes become hours, hours become days. It all just slips by. Time doesn't matter; you only start worrying about it when you need your next fix.

Then all you can think about is making money to get some more.

I had had enough.

In a way I'd made it harder on myself by insisting on doing it alone. There were all sorts of programmes and groups like Narcotics Anonymous, who would have shared the burden with me, but they didn't suit me. The difference now, of course, was that I wasn't on my own any more. I had Bob.

When I got home from the clinic, he was pleased to see me, especially as I'd stopped off at the supermarket on the way home and had a bag full of goodies that was meant to get us through the next two days. Anyone who is trying to kick an addictive habit knows what it is like. The first forty-eight hours are the hardest. You are so used to getting your 'fix' that you can't think of anything else. But at least I had Bob there with me.

That lunchtime we sat down in front of the television, had a snack together – and waited.

Probably the most famous recreation of someone 'clucking' is in the film *Trainspotting*, in which Ewan McGregor's character, Renton, decides to rid himself of his heroin addiction. He is locked in a room with some food and drink and left to get on with it. He goes through the most vile physical and mental experience you can imagine, getting the shakes, having hallucinations, being sick. All that stuff.

What I went through over the next forty-eight hours felt ten times worse than that.

The withdrawal symptoms began to kick in around twenty-four hours after I'd had my last dose of methadone. Within eight hours of that I was soaked in sweat and feeling very twitchy. By now it was the middle of the night and I should have been asleep. I did manage to nod off but it was a strange kind of sleep, full of dreams and hallucinations.

Time had no real meaning, but by the following morning I was beginning to suffer really bad migraines. As a result I found it hard to cope with any light or noise. I'd try and sit in the dark, but then I'd start dreaming or hallucinating and want to snap myself out of it. It was a vicious circle.

What I needed more than anything was

something to take my mind off it all, which was where Bob saved me.

There were times when I wondered whether Bob and I had some kind of telepathy between us. He was there all the time, hanging around me, snuggling up close when I invited him, but keeping his distance when I was having a bad time.

It was as if he knew what I was feeling. Sometimes I'd be nodding off and he would come up to me and put his face close to me, as if to say: 'You all right, mate? I'm here if you need me.' At other times he would just sit with me, purring away, rubbing his tail on me and licking my face every now and again. As I slipped in and out of a weird, hallucinatory universe, he was my anchor to reality.

By the afternoon and early evening of the second day, however, the withdrawal symptoms were really building up. The worst thing was the physical stuff. I had been warned that when you go through 'clucking' you get what's called Restless Legs Syndrome (RLS). In effect, incredibly uncomfortable, nervous pulses run through your body, so that you can't sit still. I started getting this. My legs would suddenly start kicking – it's not called kicking the habit for nothing. I think this freaked Bob out a bit.

He gave me a couple of odd, sideways looks. But he didn't desert me. He stayed there, at my side.

That night was the worst of all. One minute I was so hot I felt like I was inside a furnace. The next I'd feel ice cold. The sweat that had built up all over me would start to freeze and suddenly I'd be shivering. So then I'd have to cover up and would start burning up again. It was a horrible cycle.

Every now and again I'd have moments of clarity. At one point I remember thinking that I really understood why so many people find it so hard to kick their drug habits. It's a physical thing as well as a mental thing. The battle of wills that's going on in your brain is very one-sided. The addictive forces are certainly stronger than those that are trying to wean you off the drugs.

At another point, I was able to see the last decade and what my addiction had done to me. I saw – and sometimes smelled – the alleys and underpasses where I'd slept rough, the hostels where I'd feared for my life, the terrible things I'd done and thought about doing just to score enough heroin to get me through the next twelve hours. I saw with total clarity just how seriously addiction screws up your life.

That second night seemed to last for ever. I'd look up at the clock and it seemed, at times, as if it was moving backwards. Outside it seemed as if the darkness was getting deeper and blacker, rather than getting brighter for morning. It was horrible.

But I had my secret weapon. At one stage I was lying as still and quiet as possible, just trying to shut out the world. All of a sudden, I felt Bob clawing at my leg.

'Bob, what the hell are you doing?' I shouted.

I suspect he was worried that I was a little too still and quiet, and he was checking to make sure I was alive. He was worried about me.

Eventually, a thin, soupy grey light began to seep through the window. Morning had arrived at last. I hauled myself out of bed and looked at the clock. It was almost eight o'clock. I knew the clinic would be open by nine. I couldn't wait any longer.

I splashed some cold water on my face. It felt absolutely awful on my clammy skin. In the mirror, I could see that I looked drawn and my hair was a sweaty mess. I threw on some clothes and headed straight for the bus stop.

Getting to Camden from Tottenham at that time of the day was always a pain. Today it was the journey from hell.

As I sat on the bus, I was still having those huge temperature swings, sweating one moment, shivering the next, my limbs still twitching now and again. People were looking at me as if I was some kind of nutcase. I didn't care. I just wanted to get to the DDU.

I arrived just after nine and found the waiting room half full already. One or two people looked as rough as I felt. I wondered whether they'd been through forty-eight hours as hellish as those I'd just been through.

'Hi James, how are you feeling?' the counsellor asked.

He only needed to look at me to know the answer, of course.

'Well, you've done well to get through the last two days. That's a huge step you've taken,' he smiled.

He checked me over and gave me a tablet of Subutex.

'That should make you feel a lot better,' he said. 'Now let's start easing you off this – and out of this place completely.'

By the time I had got back to Tottenham I felt completely transformed. It was a different feeling from the one I'd had on methadone. The world seemed more vivid. I felt like I could see, hear and smell more clearly. Colours were brighter. Sounds were crisper. It was weird. It may sound strange, but I felt more alive again.

I stopped on the way and bought Bob a little toy, a squeezy mouse.

Back at the flat I made a huge fuss of him.

'We did it mate,' I said. 'We did it.'

The sense of achievement was amazing. Over the next few days, the change in my health and life in general was huge. It was as if someone had drawn back the curtains and shed some sunlight into my life.

Of course, in a way, someone had.

Chapter 12
Homeward Bound

I didn't think Bob and I could have become closer, but the experience we'd just been through together tightened our bond even more. In the days that followed, he stuck to me like a limpet, watching over me in case I slipped back.

There was no danger of that, however. I felt better than I had in years. The thought of going back to the dark habits of the past made me shiver. I had come too far now to turn back.

We even had a new patch – outside the Angel tube station in Islington, north London. It was only a few miles away from where I lived, so it was absolutely perfect and meant no more trekking through London to get to our pitch. We quickly fell in with the locals. Even the staff at the station were friendly. In every possible way, it felt like a fresh start. But there was one twist in the tale I didn't see coming . . .

It wasn't often that I got post apart from bills, so when I saw a letter in my mailbox one morning, I noticed it at once. It was an airmail envelope with a postmark: Tasmania, Australia.

It was from my mother.

We'd not been in proper contact for years. However, despite the distance that had formed between us, the letter was very chatty and warm.

'If I was to pay your air fares to Australia and back, would you come and see me?' she asked. She explained that I could come over in the Christmas holidays, which were soon coming round again.

'Let me know,' she said, signing off: 'Love, Mum.'

There was a time when I'd have thrown the letter straight into the dustbin. I'd have been defiant and stubborn and too proud to take a hand-out from my family.

But I'd changed. My head was in a different place now, so I decided to give it some thought.

It wasn't an easy decision. There were lots of pros and cons to think about.

The biggest pro, obviously, was that I'd get to

see my mother again. No matter what ups and downs we'd had over the years, she was my mother and I missed her. After all the years apart, it would be a chance to make it up to her and to put the record straight. I felt like I needed to do that.

But then there were the cons. What about Bob? Who would look after him? Did I actually want to be separated from my soulmate for weeks on end?

The answer to the first question came almost immediately.

The moment I mentioned it, Belle said she'd look after Bob at her flat. I knew she was totally trustworthy and would take care of him. But I still wondered what the effect would be on him.

I spent a few days weighing up both sides of the issue, but eventually decided I'd go. It just seemed like too good an opportunity to miss.

I had a lot to do. For a start I had to get a new passport, which wasn't easy given the way my life had fallen apart in recent years. A social worker gave me a hand and helped me organise the paperwork, including a birth certificate.

Then I needed to sort out my money. Mum had kindly offered to pay for the flight, but I still needed to show the customs people that I had money in the bank.

The flight I'd found was heading to Australia in the third week of December. So for the next three or four weeks, I worked every hour of the day in all weather. Bob came with me most days, although I left him at home when it was raining heavily. I didn't want to risk him catching a chill or getting ill before I went away. There was no way I'd be able to go to Australia if he was ill again.

I was soon saving up a bit of cash, which I kept in a little tea caddy I'd found. Slowly but surely it began to fill up. As my departure date came closer, I had enough to make the trip.

A week or so before Christmas 2008, I headed to Heathrow. I felt worried and sad. I'd said goodbye to Bob at Belle's flat. He'd not looked too concerned, but then he had no idea that I was going to be away for the best part of six weeks. I knew he'd be safe with Belle, but it still didn't stop me fretting. I really had become a paranoid parent.

It turned out to be a nightmare journey, but that was soon forgotten when I walked out of the airport in Tasmania and saw my mother there waiting for me. She gave me a couple of really long hugs. She was crying. I hugged her back tightly.

Her cottage was lovely, big and airy with a huge garden. It was surrounded by farmland with a river running by the bottom of her land. Over the next month I just hung out there, relaxing, recovering and rethinking my life.

Within a couple of weeks I felt like a different person. The stresses of London were – literally – thousands of miles away. My mum's maternal instincts kicked in and she made sure I was fed well. I could feel my strength returning. I could also sense that me and my mother were repairing our relationship.

At first we didn't talk in great depth about things, but in time I began to open up.

As I explained some of the lows I'd been through over the last ten years, my mother looked horrified.

'I guessed you weren't doing so great, but I never guessed it was that bad,' she said, close to tears.

At times she just sat there with her head in her hands.

Of course, she blamed herself. But the truth was that I had let myself down. In the end, there was no one else to blame.

'You didn't decide to sleep in cardboard boxes and get off your face on smack every night. I did,' I said at one point.

But we laughed a lot too. I often talked about Bob. I'd brought a photo of him with me, which I showed everyone and anyone who took an interest.

'He looks a smart cookie,' my mother said when she saw it.

'Oh, he is,' I said, beaming with pride. 'I don't know where I'd be now if it wasn't for Bob.'

When it came time for me to fly home, I said goodbye to my mother. I hadn't done that when I'd left years earlier, so I did it properly this time. I was sad to leave Australia, but I was dying to see Bob again. But maybe he'd forgotten me while I was away?

I needn't have worried. The minute I walked into Belle's flat his tail popped up. He bounced off her sofa and ran up to me, rushing up my arm and on to my shoulders as usual. In an instant the emotional and physical journey I'd made to the other side of the world was forgotten. It was me and Bob against the world once more.

Chapter 13

The Stationmaster

Bob and I were soon back into the old routine, sharing every aspect of our day-to-day life. But even now, after almost two years together, he was a constant source of surprise to me.

One morning, soon after I'd got back from Australia, I woke up really early. My body clock was still all over the place. I hauled myself out of bed and stepped, bleary-eyed, towards the toilet. The door was half open and I could hear a light, tinkling noise. *Weird,* I thought. When I gently nudged open the door I was greeted by a sight that left me totally speechless: Bob was squatting on the toilet seat.

Bob had clearly decided that litter trays weren't for him and that going to the toilet downstairs was too much of a hassle. So he'd worked out what he needed to do and simply copied me.

When he saw me staring at him, Bob just fired

me one of his stony looks, as if to say: 'What are you looking at? I'm only going to the loo.'

Our absence for a few weeks had definitely been noticed by the locals at the Angel. During our first week back on the pitch lots of people came up to us with big smiles. They'd say things like: 'Ah, you're back' or 'I thought you'd won the lottery.'

But people weren't always so friendly

Since the early days in Covent Garden, I'd regularly been offered money for Bob. I'd usually tell them to forget it – no chance.

Up here at the Angel I'd heard it again, from one lady in particular.

'Look, James,' she would say. 'I don't think Bob should be out on the streets. I think he should be in a nice, warm home living a better life.'

Each time she'd end the conversation with a question like: 'So how much do you want for him?'

I'd turn her down each time, at which point she'd start throwing figures at me. She'd started at £100, then gone up to £500.

Then one evening she said: 'I'll give you £1,000 for him.'

I'd just looked at her. 'Do you have children?'

'Erm, yes, as a matter of fact I do,' she spluttered.

'OK. How much for your youngest child?'

'What are you talking about?'

'How much for your youngest child?'

'I hardly think that's got anything to do—'

I cut her off. 'Actually, I think it does have a lot to do with it. As far as I'm concerned Bob is my baby. And for you to ask me whether I'd sell him is *exactly* the same as me asking you how much you want for your youngest child.'

She just stormed off. I never saw her again.

The feelings of the tube station staff were the complete opposite of this. One day I was talking to one of the ticket inspectors, Davika. She loved Bob and was chuckling at the way so many people were stopping and talking to him and taking his picture.

'He's putting Angel tube station on the map, isn't he?' she laughed.

'You should put him on the staff, like that cat in Japan who is a station master,' I said.

'I'm not sure we've got any vacancies,' she giggled.

'Well, you should at least give him an ID card or something,' I joked.

She looked at me thoughtfully and went away.

A couple of weeks later Bob and I were sitting outside the station one evening when Davika appeared again. She had a big grin on her face.

'What's up?' I said.

'Nothing, I just wanted to give Bob this,' she smiled. She then produced a laminated travel-card with Bob's photograph on it.

'That's fantastic,' I said.

'I got the picture off the Internet,' she said to my slight amazement. What the hell was Bob doing on the Internet?

'So what does it actually mean?' I asked.

'Well, it means we are all very fond of him. We think of him as part of the family.'

It took a lot of willpower to stop myself from bursting into tears.

Chapter 14
The Longest Night

While it's good to make friends, sometimes it's safer to keep your distance.

Living on the streets of London gives you really well-tuned radar when it comes to picking out people whom you want to avoid at all costs. It was during rush hour when a guy like that loomed into view.

I'd seen him once or twice before. He looked like he was sleeping rough. His skin was all red and blotchy, and his clothes were smeared in dirt. What really stuck out about him, however, was his dog: a giant Rottweiler.

The dog was with him this evening as he arrived near the tube station entrance. He sat down to talk to some other shifty-looking characters, who had been sitting there drinking lager for an hour or more. I didn't like the look of them at all.

Almost at once I could see that the Rottweiler

had spotted Bob and was straining at the lead. However, his owner seemed more interested in the lager than what his dog was doing.

I had a bad feeling about them, and wanted to get myself and Bob as far away as possible.

I began gathering up my remaining copies of *The Big Issue*. All of a sudden I heard this really loud, piercing bark. What happened next seemed as if it was in slow motion, a bad action scene from a bad action movie.

I turned round to see a flash of black and brown heading towards us. The Rottweiler was on the loose. My first instinct was to protect Bob, so I jumped in front of the dog. Before I knew it he'd run into me, bowling me over. As I fell I managed to wrap my arms around the dog and we ended up on the floor, wrestling. I was shouting and swearing, trying to get a good grip on its head so that it couldn't bite me, but the dog was too strong.

Rottweilers are powerful dogs and I have no doubt that if the fight had gone on a few seconds longer, I'd have come off second best.

'Come here, you f*****,' the owner shouted, pulling as hard as he could on the lead. He walloped the dog across the head with something blunt. In different circumstances I'd have been worried for the dog's welfare, but my main concern was Bob. He must have been terrified by what had just happened. I turned to check on him but found the spot where he'd been sitting empty. I spun around 360 degrees but there was no sign of him. He'd gone.

Suddenly, I realised what I'd done. In my effort to get away from the Rottweiler and his owner, I had unclipped Bob's lead from my belt. It had only been for a second or two while I gathered everything together, but that had been enough.

Right away I was thrown into a blind panic.

'Anyone seen Bob?' I asked, frantic and ignoring the pain in my hands where the dog had bitten me. At that moment one of my regular customers came up.

'I just saw Bob running off towards Camden Passage,' she said. 'I tried to grab his lead but he was too quick.'

I just grabbed my rucksack and ran. My chest was pounding.

I ran straight towards Camden Passage, dodging the early evening crowds milling around the pubs, bars and restaurants.

'Bob, Bob,' I kept calling, drawing looks from passers-by. 'Anyone seen a ginger tom running this way?'

They all just shrugged their shoulders.

I was beginning to despair when I met a woman towards the end of the Passage. She pointed down the road.

'I saw a cat running down the road that way,' she said. 'It was going like a rocket, veering towards the main road.'

I dashed across the road to Islington Green. Even though it was dark and I was barely able to see my hand in front of me, I hoped against hope that I might see a pair of bright eyes staring back at me.

'Bob, Bob, are you here mate?'

But apart from groans from a couple of drunks, all I could hear was the constant drone of the traffic.

It was only then that it hit me.

I'd lost him.

I was in bits. In a daze, I carried on walking down Essex Road, feeling a roller-coaster of conflicting emotions. One minute, I'd convince myself that he couldn't stray far without being found and identified. The next, a nightmare series of thoughts started pinging away in my head.

He will be OK, you'll get him back.

He's gone, you won't see him again.

I wandered up and down Essex Road for the best part of an hour. It was now pitch black and the traffic was snarled up almost all the way back to the end of Islington High Street. Without really thinking, I just started walking down Essex Road towards Dalston. My friend Belle lived in a flat about a mile away so I decided to head there.

By now the traffic had eased off. The night suddenly fell strangely quiet. For the first time I noticed that the stars were out. A few months ago I'd been staring at the stars in Tasmania. I'd told everyone that I was coming back to care for Bob. *A fine job I've done of that,* I thought bitterly.

As Belle's road came into view I was feeling close to tears. What was I going to do without him? It was then that it happened. For the first time in years I felt an overwhelming need for a fix.

I tried to bat it away, but once more my subconscious mind started fighting a battle of wills. I could feel myself thinking that if I really had lost Bob, I wouldn't be able to cope. I'd have to blot out the grief.

Belle had, like me, been fighting to stay clean for years. But I knew her flatmate still dabbled with drugs. The closer I got to her street, the more terrifying the thoughts in my head were becoming.

By the time I reached Belle's house, it was nearly 10 p.m. I had been wandering the streets for a couple of hours. In the distance, sirens were wailing once more as police made their way to another stabbing or punch up in a pub. I couldn't have cared less.

As I walked up the path to the dimly lit front door I spotted a shape sitting quietly in the shadows to the side of the building. It was a cat, but I'd given up hope by now and just assumed it was another stray, sheltering from the cold. But then I saw his face, that face.

'Bob!'

He let out a plaintive meow, just like the one in the hallway three years ago, as if to say: 'Where have you been? I've been waiting here for ages.'

I scooped him up and held him close.

'You are going to be the death of me if you keep running away like that,' I said, my mind scrambling to work out how he'd got here.

It must be a mile and a half from our pitch at the Angel. How long had he been here? Had he really walked all the way? But none of that mattered now. As I carried on making a fuss of him, he licked my hand, his tongue as rough as sandpaper. He rubbed his face against mine and curled his tail.

I rang Belle's doorbell and she invited me in. My mood had been transformed from despair to delight. I was on top of the world.

Belle's flatmate was also there.

'Want something to celebrate?' she said, smiling, knowingly.

'No, I'm fine thanks,' I said, hugging Bob to me. 'Just a beer would be great.'

Bob didn't need drugs to get through the night. He just needed his companion: me. And at that moment I decided that was all I needed too. All I needed was Bob. Not just tonight, but for as long as I had the honour of having him in my life.

Chapter 15

Bob, *The Big Issue* Cat

Bob and I were soon back to our old routine, but things were about to change – for the better.

One March evening I was checking that I had enough magazines left to cope with the rush hour, when I saw out of the corner of my eye that a group of kids had gathered around us. They were teenagers I guessed, three boys and a couple of girls. They looked Spanish, or maybe Latin American.

'Ah, *si* Bob,' said one teenage girl.

'*Si, si.* Bob Ze Beeg Issew Cat,' said another.

Weird, I thought to myself. *How do they know his name is Bob? He doesn't wear a name tag. And what do they mean by* The Big Issue *Cat*?

I became curious. I had to speak to them.

'Sorry, hope you don't mind me asking, but how do you know Bob?' I said, in the hope that one of them spoke English.

Fortunately a young boy replied. 'Oh, we see

him on YouTube,' he smiled. 'Bob is very popular, yes?'

'Is he?' I said. 'Where are you from?'

'*España*, Spain.'

'So Bob's popular in Spain?'

'*Si, si*,' said another one of the boys. '*Bob es una estrella en España*. Bob is a star in Spain.'

I was shocked.

I knew that lots of people had taken photographs of Bob over the years. A couple of people had filmed him too, some with their phones, others with proper video cameras. Who could have shot a film that was now on YouTube?

The following morning I headed down to the local library with Bob and used a public computer to go online.

To my surprise, when I did a search there was not one, but two films.

'Hey Bob, look, he was right. You are a star on YouTube.'

He hadn't been terribly interested until that point. But when I clicked on the first video and saw and heard myself talking, he jumped on to the keyboard and popped his face right up against the screen.

The first film, *Bobcat and I*, had been shot by a film student. The second, *Bob* The Big Issue

Cat was by a Russian guy. This must have been the one that the Spanish students had seen. It had had tens of thousands of hits. I was gob-smacked.

The feeling that Bob was becoming some kind of celebrity had been building for a while. A few weeks ago, we had featured in a local newspaper. I'd even been approached by an American agent, who asked me whether I'd thought about writing a book about me and Bob. As if!

But the Spanish teenagers made me realise something. Bob was becoming a feline star!

On one of the films, I had said that Bob had saved my life. When I first heard it I thought it sounded like a bit too much, a bit of an exaggeration. But as I walked away from the library it began to sink in: it was true, he really had.

In the two years since I'd found him sitting in that half-lit hallway, Bob had transformed my world. Back then I'd been a recovering heroin addict living a hand-to-mouth existence. I was in my late twenties, and yet I had no real direction or purpose in life. I'd lost contact with my family and barely had a friend in the world. Now all that had changed.

Not only had I faced my past, but I'd finally laid down some roots. It might not have seemed much to most people, but my little flat in Tottenham had given me the kind of security and stability that I'd always craved. And my battle with drugs was finally drawing to a close. That would not have happened if it hadn't been for Bob.

I believe in karma, the idea that what goes around comes around. Sometimes I wonder whether Bob is my reward for having done something good, somewhere in my troubled life.

But it's really pretty simple. Bob is my best mate and he's guided me towards a different – and a better – way of life. He doesn't demand anything complicated or difficult in return. He just needs me to take care of him. And that's what I do.

Everybody needs a break. Everybody deserves that second chance. Bob and I have taken ours . . .

Read the latest news and stories from James and Bob at www.facebook.co.uk/StreetCatBob and at Bob's very own Twitter site: @StreetCatBob

'A heart-warming tale with a message of hope'
Daily Mail

'An instantly bestselling memoir that, beside its heart-warming tale of their friendship, offers an insight into the injustice of life on the streets that's by turns frustrating and life-affirming.'
The Times

The moving, uplifting true story of an unlikely friendship between a man on the streets and the ginger cat who adopts him and helps him heal his life.

'Close proximity to animals does wonders for your mental health. Close proximity to this book will do wonders for it, too.'
Daily Mail

The sequel to the bestselling tale A STREET CAT NAMED BOB, THE WORLD ACCORDING TO BOB continues the remarkable adventures of James and Bob showing – through new stories – how Bob's extraordinary street wisdom has shown James the meaning of friendship, loyalty, trust – and happiness.

Books in the Series

Available in paperback, ebook and from your local library

Amy's Diary	Maureen Lee
Beyond the Bounty	Tony Parsons
Bloody Valentine	James Patterson
Blackout	Emily Barr
Chickenfeed	Minette Walters
Cleanskin	Val McDermid
The Cleverness of Ladies	Alexander McCall Smith
Clouded Vision	Linwood Barclay
A Cool Head	Ian Rankin
A Cruel Fate	Lindsey Davis
The Dare	John Boyne
Dead Man Talking	Roddy Doyle
Doctor Who: Code of the Krillitanes	Justin Richards
Doctor Who: Magic of the Angels	Jacqueline Rayner
Doctor Who: Revenge of the Judoon	Terrance Dicks
Doctor Who: The Silurian Gift	Mike Tucker
Doctor Who: The Sontaran Games	Jacqueline Rayner
A Dreadful Murder	Minette Walters
A Dream Come True	Maureen Lee
The Escape	Lynda La Plante
Follow Me	Sheila O'Flanagan
Four Warned	Jeffrey Archer
Full House	Maeve Binchy
Get the Life You Really Want	James Caan
The Grey Man	Andy McNab
Hello Mum	Bernardine Evaristo

Hidden	Barbara Taylor Bradford
How to Change Your Life in 7 Steps	John Bird
Humble Pie	Gordon Ramsay
Jack and Jill	Lucy Cavendish
Kung Fu Trip	Benjamin Zephaniah
Last Night Another Soldier	Andy McNab
Life's New Hurdles	Colin Jackson
Life's Too Short	Val McDermid, Editor
The Little One	Lynda La Plante
Love is Blind	Kathy Lette
Men at Work	Mike Gayle
Money Magic	Alvin Hall
One Good Turn	Chris Ryan
Out of the Dark	Adèle Geras
Paris for One	Jojo Moyes
The Perfect Holiday	Cathy Kelly
The Perfect Murder	Peter James
Pictures Or It Didn't Happen	Sophie Hannah
Quantum of Tweed: The Man with the Nissan Micra	Conn Iggulden
Red for Revenge	Fanny Blake
Rules for Dating a Romantic Hero	Harriet Evans
A Sea Change	Veronica Henry
Star Sullivan	Maeve Binchy
Street Cat Bob	James Bowen
The 10 Keys to Success	John Bird
Tackling Life	Charlie Oatway
Today Everything Changes	Andy McNab
Traitors of the Tower	Alison Weir
Trouble on the Heath	Terry Jones
Twenty Tales from the War Zone	John Simpson
We Won the Lottery	Danny Buckland
Wrong Time, Wrong Place	Simon Kernick

Quick Reads are brilliant short new books written by bestselling writers to help people discover the joys of reading for pleasure.

Find out more at **www.quickreads.org.uk**

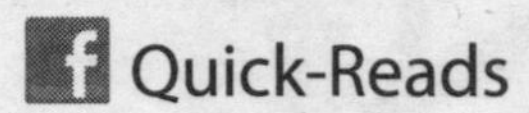

We would like to thank all our funders:

We would also like to thank all our partners in the Quick Reads project for their help and support: NIACE, unionlearn, National Book Tokens, The Reading Agency, National Literacy Trust, Welsh Books Council, The Big Plus Scotland, DELNI, NALA

At Quick Reads, World Book Day and World Book Night we want to encourage everyone in the UK and Ireland to read more and discover the joy of books.

World Book Day is on 5 March 2015
Find out more at **www.worldbookday.com**

World Book Night is on 23 April 2015
Find out more at **www.worldbooknight.org**

Why not start a reading group?

If you have enjoyed this book, why not share your next Quick Read with friends, colleagues, or neighbours.

A reading group is a great way to get the most out of a book and is easy to arrange. All you need is a group of people, a place to meet and a date and time that works for everyone.

Use the first meeting to decide which book to read first and how the group will operate. Conversation doesn't have to stick rigidly to the book. Here are some suggested themes for discussions:

- How important was the plot?
- What messages are in the book?
- Discuss the characters – were they believable and could you relate to them?
- How important was the setting to the story?
- Are the themes timeless?
- Personal reactions – what did you like or not like about the book?

There is a free toolkit with lots of ideas to help you run a Quick Reads reading group at **www.quickreads.org.uk**

Share your experiences of your group on Twitter @Quick_Reads

For more ideas, offers and groups to join visit Reading Groups for Everyone at **www.readingagency.org.uk/readinggroups**

Enjoy this book?

Find out about all the others at **www.quickreads.org.uk**

For Quick Reads audio clips as well as videos and ideas to help you enjoy reading visit the BBC's Skillswise website **www.bbc.co.uk/quickreads**

Skillswise

Join the Reading Agency's Six Book Challenge at **www.readingagency.org.uk/sixbookchallenge**

THE READING AGENCY

Find more books for new readers at
www.newisland.ie
www.barringtonstoke.co.uk

Free courses to develop your skills are available in your local area. To find out more phone 0800 100 900.

For more information on developing your skills in Scotland visit **www.thebigplus.com**

Want to read more? Join your local library. You can borrow books for free and take part in inspiring reading activities.